LABYRINTH of SONGS
Vol. 1 Path of Tezcatlipoca

LABYRINTH of SONGS

Vol. 1 Path of Tezcatlipoca

Poems By
Jorge Montaño

RIOT OF ROSES
PUBLISHING HOUSE
SEJATNGA
UNCEDED TONGVA TERRITORY
SOUTH WHITTIER, CALIFORNIA

Labyrinth of Songs Vol. 1: Path of Tezcatlipoca
Copyright © 2024, Jorge Montaño

ISBN (paperback): 978-1-961717-20-6
ISBN (ebook): 978-1-961717-21-3
Library of Congress Control Number: 2024943923

Cover Art© Rick Ortega 2024

First Edition, 2024

To request permissions, you may contact the Publisher
at riotofrosesllc@gmail.com

Printed in the United States of America.
www.riotofrosespublishinghouse.com
Cover design by Jacob Ortega
Layout design by Waseem Aziz at arrowupz.com
Edited by Brenda Vaca

Advance Praise

Through his poems, Jorge Montaño takes us on a journey through our ancestral beginnings, reminding us of our connection to Mother Earth and our natural adherence to the Four Directions. Every poem we encounter in his Labyrinth of Songs, acts as a spiritual cleanse that ultimately leads us to transformation, to rebirth.

– **Obed Silva,** English Professor at East Los Angeles College and Author of The Death of My Father the Pope

Jorge Montaño is a warrior poet whose eloquent writing is reminiscent of ancient Mesoamerican storytelling. As an artist, I can visualize the meaningful metaphors that inspire the heart and mind into creativity, as he reiterates the spirituality of a pre-Colombian past into a modern day masterpiece of flower and song.

– **Rick Ortega,** Visual Artist

For years I have had the pleasure of witnessing the growth of Jorge Montaño as he has honed his craft as a poet and a passionate student and emissary for the wisdom of our people. In this book, Jorge has brought together the most stunning reflections on the nature of consciousness, spiritual growth and evolution, and the brilliant teachings our Toltekatl ancestors have passed onto us of each of these. This book is a powerful invitation to explore the mystery of existence through the power of words and the willingness to wonder at the depth of wisdom that is alive in our ancestral lineage.

~ Dr. Oscar C. Pérez, Bestselling Author of The Flowering War: Toltec Teachings on Healing Ancestral Trauma, Overcoming Your Internal Enemies, and Fulfilling Your Life Purpose

Contents

Book of Calli

Book of Cuetzpalin

Book of Coatl

BOOK OF CIPACTLI

Instinct

Tlahuizlampa

●

The Beginning

Within the exhale of this enclosure

Pulsates the beginning

Uncertainty awakens

Pierced are the remnants of broken shadows

Within the expansion of a captured thought

It is light that recreates itself

Fear dwindles into fading smoke

Through the appetite to live

Through the womb of a thousand mouths

The soul begins its descent

Into my hands

Into my thoughts

Through gratitude

My eyes welcome light

The Haze

A haze of blurred faces

Scream through noises of desire

Pieces of broken words

Pant for the ink of a dormant quill

Sheets of unborn pages

Tumble in crumbled thought

Ocean aroused in restlessness

Tossed around by a need to write

Breath enters a collapsing spark

Awareness flickers into a spiraling plunge

Birth swallowed by the void of light

Hunger tastes the drops of faith

I am found in spirit

I am masked in scales of paint

I am smeared in voiceless stains

I am scribbled upon muted stone

I am scattered amongst the timeless sand

Great Ancestor

Great ancestor

Ancient Cipactli

Our origins coincide with the cosmos

Our beginnings take shape from desire

You were once untamed

As you hunted through the ocean of space

Yet now

You are the primal womb

Which begets survival

An instinct that craves light

An intuition multiplied into living cells

An evolution of species

I have sprouted from the scales of your flesh

You are every lifeform

You are every micro-organism

You are everyone of us

Our blood carries your face

Filled is our communion

By the awareness which relates

To this archaic Providence

●●●●

Light and Life

I search for light

Through the currents of thought

Through the wavering silence

Through my own quiet explosions

I search for life

Where emptiness is not all that empty

Where the stillness surrounds me

Where emotion gladdens me with the ability

To dive into myself

———

Made of the Cosmos

I am made of cosmic vitality

Of sustained energy

A movement that desires

A calling upon consciousness

I am a momentum of my tonalli

I am bound to the Creator

I am synchronized with purpose

I am rooted to a destiny

A soul that is never beyond me

Maternal Love

She explodes with joy

The caves of terrestrial passage sing unto the night

The flowers have heard their mother's call

The earth has given forth light

The silence shivers with an awakening

Ancient is her deepest secrets

To give is our freedom

To love is our common bond

And to comfort each other is the power eternal

Creative Elements

Creator of fragmented beginnings

Energy of our sustenance

You are at the center

Creative elements orbit your song

The humming of the Universe is inhaled

Exhaled are the stars

As they are caught upon the fabric of space

Upon the dark waves of eternal ambience

An ocean of time

Emanating from the hunger

That I hold inside

Centered by Existence

Centered by existence

Filled with the need to be alive

Devouring all elements of creation

Hunted and divided by both chaos and order

From inside her core

From within has the creature turned out

Spinning and dangling

From divine threads the earth takes form

The Lord of Existence touches her skin with sustenance

His warmth has made the soil fertile

Life is given unto their descendants

Only the rooted

Will be sustained by their light

●●●●

Faceless Light

Centered by forgetting myself

Who I was hovers above into feathered dust

Scattered stars into tired silence

I remain focused

Grasping the heart of existence

Devouring its mysteries as they awaken

Unknown is the path which descends

Out of the celestial waters

Inverted by obscured direction

I am prepared to consume my first breath

I am a song in search of a face

A faceless light of dreams unwritten

Inside of Me

Outside of me

Outside of you

Outside of us

We are covered with beginnings

We are held by whispers of inception

We are fed energies of ancient growing

We are nurtured by the Lord of Our Existence

We are told to survive our silence

We are given everything needed

We are a life born from a death

Inside of us

Inside of you

 Inside of me

Breathes a thought

A fire within an empty room

A Greater Light

That which is consumed

Is absorbed into the purpose

Of a greater light

When fed by knowledge

Balance reflects action

Darkness cannot be

As long as there is breath

Swallowed is the abyss

Yet the soul will find its freedom

Movement is inevitable

There was once this Great creature

Who now pours out life

All Is Energy

Beneath the rays of the speaking sun

All is touched by energy

Through the many mouths of Cipactli

All sprout from energy

Within stone and bone

Conserved is the hardening of energy

Words become the songs of heightened energy

Dance becomes aroused by Divine energy

Sacred fire is kindled in the silence of trapped energy

Teotl translates into creative energy

Reverence of energy becomes Creator

All is energy

All is living

I seek no longer

I feel its warmth upon my face

Light Bearer

Light unknown

Spark ripples the silence

Bursting glow

Humbled flame

It dares not consume the darkness

Its warmth calls me to realize

Its fire transcends me

We are gathered into awakening

The earth opens her primal caves

Mouths of hungry obsidian

Teeth stained with bleeding light

Into the depths are thrown sacrificed thoughts

Life is poured into the absolute

Until space and time vanish

Bundled inside the heart of Omeyocan

BOOK OF EHECATL

Realization

Mictlampa

●

Let Go

I reach out to touch the face of the sky

Without looking

Without hands

With only my ears

With only listening

Around me, under me and over me

All is weightless

Scales of time fall onto deserted hours

Of moments made hollow

Of plumage made spoken

I am taken by the whispering wind

Fluent voice captured by simplicity

Into all directions my wings stretch

As the secret beckons me

To let go

●●

The Poet Is Born

Whisperings uncoil from humming vibrations

Ringings bounce upon speaking drums

Voices spiral into catacombs of thought

Spells broken from a rattles dance

Night diluted in wavering dream

Skies unfold into breath of life

Spirit calls the chosen hour

The conch shell awakens

The poet is born

Feathered songs carve into the painted leaves

As childlike symbols inscribe their knowledge

Within the pause of sands untouched

Where hesitant waves unfurl

Into the opening of themselves

I am spoken by the life within me

I am whispered by the Soul

I am the wind

I walk in the spirit of Its word

Voices Of Old

Voices of old

Once spoke into the rising fire

Into the painted flowers filled by the east

Here elder songs instruct their descendants

To understand the words between the ethers

So that there is no confusion

So that truth opens not the door for ignorance

But for the song of endurance

These voices can still be heard

As brother tree recites from the pages of his leaves

Where the humming of bees gathers before their queen

Where the fire sets upon its own silence

Where lectures the moon of how dreams cannot be undone

Gratitude

Gratitude is the life force of reverence

The honoring of sky and earth

Of fire and water

Of movement and stillness

This is the inhaling reason of acceptance

Gratitude serves to shelter our thoughts

From the corrupt nature of indulgence

Overconsumption has its methods

Of trapping the moment into arrogance

But it is the grateful attitude

Which guides our steps

Through a field of broken sand

Beneath our feet time gathers and it scatters

Our knowing raises us

It helps us to hover

Weightless

Here we are without harming the seeds

Know what brings you despair

Know what makes your senses dance

Know what brings you fear

Know what makes you feel warm

Use this knowledge

To push the clouds

Where drought hides from rain

Know that you can breathe life

Into the creation of consciousness

Spoken Light

Sweeping breath

Heard to cast medicine

Sage scented in ghostlike prayer

Quixotic gestures of possibilities

Untouched yet attainable

Path cleared of hindered labyrinth

Doubt rebuked into ripples of certainty

Dreams filtered through prisms of faith

I am amongst the plumage of sanctified colors

My eyes rise into sighs of life

Thought sleeps not in spoken light

Truth

Truth cannot be held in words

Says the wind

As tired pages are stripped off

From the bibles of murdered trees

For leaves faded of life

Are swallowed by the unknown motion

Which concludes with answers untold

Truth is broken into thousands of kisses

And pressed against the lips of falling moments

Essence of Wisdom

Broken leaves of jigsaw pieces

Winding breath into spiral thought

Written hours conceived in timeless space

Wind unmasked in eternal love

Sacrifice stroked while fire speaks

Soul embraced in creative dance

Connected in twisted strands

Of cosmic dreams in fetal cave

Drumming

Song unfolding

Kept silent for far too long

Stirred ink of ancestral blood

They whisper through the waters

They hum through chanting words

Life is bound

Life is sound

It is Wisdom which fills the hollow of earth

It is insight which fuels the fires

It is knowledge which oxygenates liquid light

It is inspiration which carries the contemplated

To the fields of understanding

All serve to create the seed of divine expression

All are created to help sow the essence of Wisdom

Through My Hands

Through my hands

Through the rustling of leaves

Through the plumage of shedding serpents

Ehecatl whispers into the doors of consciousness

The Great Wind awakens my senses

I can smell fragrance in the air

I can hear the echoes of forever

I can interpret the uncontainable

Through words written

I can transcend the moment

Life Giver

Life giver

Breath of life

Into my bones have you spoken

From the beds of Mictlampa

I rise

I ascend through cosmic mist

A ghost made of drops of wine

An intoxicated spirit wearing its mask of jade

I am no longer I

But a breath beyond me

Amongst ancestor song

A singing voice of the ancient father

Opened Passage

Opened passage

Living breath spinning

Articulating pages rooted in thought

Spirals of song permitting reverence

As spirits carve into a mask of dust

Sacredness therein

Inside my chest

Inside my mind

Inside each word

Seeds which call forth gratitude

It is the awareness of wisdom which holds me intact

Wisdoms Breath

Thickened shroud of cosmic dust

Voice unheard through illusions of smoke

Pleads of movement in spinning stillness

Crowded sky seeks to undress

Confused has sleep opened its arms

Perception is felt to invoke the air

Awakened has thought found escape

Scented has Spirit revealed itself

Faceless no longer

As wisdom breathes life upon the earth

Purpose

My body awakens from a non-existence

Out of a gathering of dust and stone

Rises the parables of living song

There is no curse

There is no mistake

There is only purpose

The wind makes music

From the carved instruments of reverent thoughts

Whisperings of the Heart

Both sun and moon are speaking

Light and dream entwine

Words bundle inside the voice of sage

Guidance is in the warmth of the wind

Omecihuatl, Ometecuhtli

Lady and Lord of Duality

Space and time are honored

In prayer

In song

In the fragrance of love

There is a howling

And it has brought me here

To Omeyocan

Where the breath of life spirals

Where smoke awakens thought

Where sacred ground is found

In the whisperings of the heart

BOOK OF CALLI

Shelter

Cihuatlampa

●

Temple of Love

Walk through your mind

There in every chamber dwell your thoughts

Go in without discomfort

Without fear

Converse with those ideas' worth speaking with

And seek out what stench was left by ignorance

Throw out the trash

Wash the floors

And realize the sacred space within you

There is a feeling of wholeness when each door is opened

When each room entered

When each window is wiped clean

Your mind

Your heart

Your temple becomes sanctified by Spirit and Light

Of all things to keep is your dignity

Of all things to give is your compassion

Clarity is the result when these are in balance

Become a thought of energy

And love will follow

Sacred Mountain

The sacred mountain, temple of the creators

Stone stairways, carved with celestial images

From the foothill to the apex

Trees announce their breath

Words translate through angelic birds

Feathered songs ever-so-watching

To ascend is only by way of inspiration

Children run without tiring

Streams ripple into broken waterfalls

Flowers bathe in the reflection of the glistening light

My heart dwells within this great house

As the night drums into speaking dreams

Through me

Both sky and earth become one

Fountain of Fire

From the rugged hills of bronze clay

Chiseled dust is caught and woven into flesh

Chosen of ancient stone

Structured into skeletal strength

Temple in which is contained the holy fire

Where ancestral streams

Of voices that flow through my blood

Here drums the unending wisdom

As music fills each living cell

Each drop sent through the fountain of the heart

Silence beckons me

To listen

To translate confusion into understanding

Vessel of Emotion

Emotion steers the vessel

Careful not to awaken torment

It is the soothing voice that the waters listen for

Walk with care

Speak through the caress of words

I see pain being washed off

A waterfall shelters me from fear

There it goes down stream

Away from the temple of bone

Within, the soul kisses my thoughts

And I too, will speak of light

—

House of the Creator

House of bone painted in flesh

House of spirit echoes in ancient breath

House of ancestral blood in sacred fire

House of innocence bathed in jade mist

House of expression

Place where cosmic energies submerge to consecrate

To converse

To create

In the Teocalli

In the House of the Creator

Mind Renewed

A trail of broken rock

Residue of borrowed thoughts

Etched memoirs of tired dreams

Leaning into a relic draped in eroded stone

Gathered inside of bundled arms

Falling forward

Centered amidst abandoned silence

Raising pillars of reconstruction

Movement kindled

Windows wiped from dust

A Soul invoked through voice of old

Presence sparking warmth

Sage smoke blessing the doors

This is the path of a mind renewed

Rise Eagle Warriors

House buried within the seeds

Dwelling of our ancestors

House del Yaqui

House del Comanche

House del Apache

House del Navajo

House del Mexica

House of their descendants

The lands have been gated

Prisons filled with children bound to empty rights

Voices of Spirits demanding their release

The mission bell tower is crumbling

Occupied minds are remembered

The high courts of Earth and Sky have ruled in our favor!

Rise, young Eagle Warriors!

Rise, so that the sun can see your brown faces

Sacred Fields

An invisible wind has called to me

A thought has been provoked

My heart is drumming

My breath is singing

Scented are these words

As they intertwine into verse

They are praying for our children

They are seeking for light

Illumination for their minds to awaken

For they must also sing

They must also be allowed to drum

They must stand to walk

Walk gently upon sacred fields

Of an ancient house covered in plumage

I am where all are centered into one

I am feeling the beautiful earth

She is moving beneath my feet

I am hearing whispers in the sky

He is opening into light

Our descendants will dance once again

Templo del Momento

Mi cuerpo

Templo del espíritu

Sacred domain of divine mystery

Fuente hecho en escultura cósmica

Heart drumming from elders' song

Mi alma bailando alrededor del fuego

Fire within

Drawing breath from life

La palabra de los vientos tomando refugio

Here it recites a riddle as it migrates through the corridors

Antes que se vaya tengo que resolver su misterio

I must hurry! No, I must realize!

Solo tengo este momento

Tepeyollotl

Doors open

The night sky is poured out

From a temple upon a shadowed peak

From the caves that echo through Tepeyollotl

Windows are made to glow in starlight

My thoughts

They are embraced by Spirit

They are like little creatures dressed in nocturnal bliss

Not knowing that truth rises up from dreams

They never sleep

They wait to pounce upon the sun

They whisper to each other

Stories of love

Myths of how one day a light will free them

How this moment could exist

If only the mountain closes its eyes once again

And only then will the twilight

Guide us through the labyrinth

Face to Face

Face to face

Past and present

Ancestor ghost

And modern-day Chicano

Both watching into the hollow of the other

Into the eyes of multi-dimensional connection

Except it is the ghost who beholds the future

Once unseen

Yet within the chambers of his tomorrow

And it is I

Who steps into the energies of sheltered knowledge

A temple of ancient stone

Body protected by magic

The Heart-Of-The-Mountain

Tepeyollotl surrounds the structure of cosmic exchange

As does the night's embrace

As stars gaze into my mind

As does the dream inside the realization

Of its own presence

Two from One

Fire is realized when two emerge from one

One truth is balanced by two sides

One sound is performed by both breath and instrument

Divine integrity is held by day and night

Here is my temple

Held and shaped by the hands of twilight

Amidst the four Tezcatlipocas

Pillars of the Sky-That-Is-The-Place-Of-The-Creators

Sanctuary upon the peaks of Tepeyollotl

Where thought and sacrifice are fused in transparency

Unbroken by the shaking of Tlaltipac

House of Spirit

House of Soul

Affirmation at the gates of Omeyocan

Temple of the Sky, House of the Earth

The Night Wind whispers

Energy venerates through a verb of light

Celestial skin protrudes into a starlit passage

Sacrificed space kissed by sacred breath

Temple of the Sky

Keeper of unborn Creators

Fire carved symbols buried inside the heart

You have impregnated her

The Earth trembles

Drizzled drops fill the cup of fertile caves

Blessed womb stirring creation

Mountains of chameleon trees sing into blossoms of Cenzontles

Walls of fragrance

Heart drumming

Waters of jade flowing

House of the Earth

Giver of rising messengers

Both flower and song reside within

Solitude lurks without being able to find them

Strength awaits to be heard

Life longs to be seen

BOOK OF CUETZPALIN

Dreams

Huitzlampa

●

Trees of Huehuecoyotl

In the sanctum layered of sacred thought

A timeless presence carves into muted laughter

The eyes of ghosts are scattered

Inebriated by the chanting of dreaming trees

They pray

They raise their tired limbs

They plead with the wind

As discolored leaves find themselves

In the hands of phantom scribes

Huehuecoyotl is seen

He is pounding against their sleeping trunks

He is awakening them

Before the ancients can finish their song

The Lizard

Deep within this reality

Springs up another truth

It is the Cuetzpalin who crawls into my sleep

She portrays an unspoken scene

A message through a dream

A whispering haze introduces a night's end

Scented are the words of dreams undressed

Seductive winds wrap my thoughts with knowing

Transparent color of gardens unfolding

Of dried riverbeds soaked with light

Of trees rooted inside the seats of shadows

My eyes search within as well as gaze out

Inside the truth of illusion

And upon the illusion of truth

I am between worlds

I dare not ignore the possibility of losing myself

My eyes are closed

The search begins for Cuetzpalin

The path descends into the deep

The gates are buried in moments forgotten

Huehuecoyotl, the old coyotl

He is laughing behind the weeds of sorrow

He is holding broken wings

Feathers scatter into singing flowers

And sure enough

The vision empties into fading whispers

Voices speckled on the eyes of a lizard

Mask of Dreams

In a dream

The day awakens behind a mask

A vibe acts out its divine personality

That of a tired coyotl

Or maybe of a playful ocelotl

The moon with her twilight stare

Commences to seduce the painted stage

As she whispers through her disguise

In the wavering silhouette of a priestess

She is a poetess casting spells

Upon the leaves of forgotten trees

Moonlight spills

All spiral into whirlwinds of dance

Inverted subconscious funnels into thoughts

Broken of silence

Story unleashed of unique awareness

Nothing quiets except for the dawn

Where a new mask appears

Behind every flowering song

A new dream

Where pieces of ancient words

Run rampant

While their gaze becomes as hunters

Seekers of what hides within the labyrinth

The Undefeated

Waters flow into the corners of spinning thoughts

Wounded warriors submerged beneath the sparks of dreams

Washed of their shame

Made pure among the buried stones

Of those found reborn

Of those lost within the labyrinth of illusion

Here are the souls of rising mist

And here are those recreated

Gathered by the hands of a manifested song

Cascading light from the words of the undefeated

Singing Labyrinth

Spinning stars fall into grains of sand

Breath buried in Creators song

Lucid flame wrinkle inside of shrinking palms

Waters awaken from the stirring of consciousness

Tearing eyes open

As visions pour out the melting sun

Golden mist of violet haze

Rise from the sleep of dust and ash

I am reduced from endless dance

I seek for the voice of creation

The smeared illusion of unrealized emptiness

It is stroked by the unconscious palm of dreaming words

Unknown is the chalice of destinies

Offerings stained by bleeding skies

Into the echoes of my heart

Into the temple of my ancestors

Where healing burns into feathered smoke

There are confirmed my Creators

There they speak of what has not yet spoken

Of what has been gathered by sacrificed hands

I am of earth

I am of air

I am of fire

I am of water

I am the depths rising into a singing labyrinth

Abandoned Drum

A distant howl undresses a dream

A shroud of velvet smoke welcomes my descent

I am inside a plumed consciousness

Where my presence is held by midnight fire

Unknowing of the reality that whispers

It speaks of a love that rages through me

It speaks of she as being the cause

She who carries me to mingle with the caress of the clouds

The gathering skies could not help but to gently cry

The drops of solace find the remains of a coyotl

Within the trench of broken seeds

It is here where thirst is quenched

Where life returns

Into the hollow of an abandoned drum

Creators Unborn

You pour inside of me your sight

Your eyes seek not a way out

They sift through the piles of broken dreams

Disturbed are spirits of the unwritten

Awoken are the wounds by your caress

Here opens a room, a tomb, a womb

Released are the sounds of deep space

I embrace your visit with flowers

It is my soul that you chase within a house made of words

The dream comes to whisper

Of what the eyes cannot see

It is a surfacing bubble bursting in my grasp

It is a portal hidden behind the face of Creators unborn

Gaze of Thoughts

Dreams change through choices made

From spirals found in whispering depths

They crawl out from the gaze of thoughts

Mind undressed by illusions touch

Visions born through silent womb

Night awakens with different eyes

Movement bound in buried time

Words escape from a darkness torn by destiny

What Surrounds Me?

What surrounds me?

Shadows scattered into consequence

Choices made to awaken the unknowing

They stretch out into a quiet shatter

Where no one can see

My face is hidden from their eyes

I realize illusion

Yet love can feel my reality

Truth generated

From the heart which drums inside me

No other can feel this rhythm

Only the moon with her golden bells

It is an energy which flows into time

Be that of pain

Be that of love

But better for creation

Be that of self-sacrifice

Imagine a dream that gives without holding back

Imagine abundance of light

Can you hear her?

The earth is whispering

The night is breaking

===

A Crashing Silence

I am floating upon a crashing silence

Sleep runs and hides behind voiceless shadows

Words rise into the deepening cosmos

My spirit opens wide the scaled gates

Thoughts bound in the caress of bleeding stars

The spinning earth

The moaning foghorn

The ant tunneling through the echoes of space

The creaking walls

Ancestors walking on broken leaves

Awareness keeps me away from the blindfolds of sleep

While the breathing night watches me roll around

I am not here nor there

I am floating upon a crashing silence

Temporary Enclosure

It hovers over my presence

My face reflects on itself

A dream bridges together two sides

I cross to meet myself

Braided is spirit and flesh

At a blurred horizon of sky and earth

Awareness and confusion become one

I realize my movements, yet my mind feels only words

The morning sings

Light fills my eyes while the night awakens

It is untouched by my thoughts

It hides inside its temporary enclosure

The Desert Heat

From inside the crumbling vapors of desert heat

Rise the spires of Mayahuel

Here where water has forgotten me

Is my throat being quenched by the bleeding maguey

From her agua miél

I am being fed her hypnosis

I am made still

My movements are found in thought

Through flourishing tropics

Through the amazonian painted jungle

Through tangled vines of mist covered visions

My Senses mesmerized by fragrant vibrations

My thoughts are found in movement

In and out of sight

Through the plumage of the red and blue macaw

I am wrapped within a feathered embrace

A horizon unfinished through camouflaged eyes

It is my Soul that is in entranced

By the Spirit of singing hallucinations

Flowering Songs

An autumn portal waits for what whispers a dying day

Leaves of tired skin held upon the wells of half-closed eyes

Physical limitation is transcended

Solid walls of confinement fade

Dream spills over mortal gates

Undisturbed is the environment which sleeps

Obsidian root caressed by silk digging through the softened soil

Shadows poured over the naked hills of forsaken hours

Forgotten by everyone except the waning moon

She too dissolves like a ghost that is taken by the wind

Expansion of spirit succeeds

Enraptured energy implodes into inverted springs

Consciousness unlocked as does steam from fire

Creators in silhouette of timeless jade

Father-Mother inseparable

Abiding in the center of flowering songs

BOOK OF COATL

Rebirth

Tlahuitzlampa

●

Mother of the Sun

To see is to hear

To smell is to taste

To touch is to speak

One reacts from the other

There is a kindness invoked

She stands at the gates

Where a reverence is taught

to the whisperings that pass through

This guardian cowards not

Where forbidden is the rage of doubt

She is Mother of the sun

Divine creator of every face

She is within me

She is the benevolence imposed

At the moment of awakening

My eyes pierce through the darkness

They gaze upon the winding river of shimmering light

My ears sift through the piles of vibrant noise

Where thought chases the spirit of time

Here the scent of flowered mist fills my mind

An indulgence drinks from sentient wine

My hands reach into obsidian pools

The caress converses with the echoes of breathing stars

Awakened Skies

Stone of awakened skies

Carved face with celestial eyes

Integrated feathers open wide

Thoughts of light transform inside

Breath spoken through wisdoms motion

Shadows broken by quetzal plumage

Demons rattled in creative presence

Knowledge stumbles among the wingless

Temporal pleasures reorganize

Energies summon warriors to rise

Precious light taking captive of my disguise

Words uncovered from life realized

Spirit of awakened skies

Scented voice with celestial eyes

Integrated feathers open wide

Thoughts of light transform inside

The Waking Hour

Warmth counsels the questions of doubt

Cold stillness melts into drops of a realized caress

Rising voices of cascabeles echo through enclosed space

A fire serpent kindles the count of time

Death is pushed out by the wisdom of life

Confusion falls like the scales of an awakened song

Presence burning

As night dilutes into the melting of moments

Bathed within a coiled fire

Thrusting forth

Emptied from the womb of yesterday

My eyes reach forth

From shedding skin

From serpent womb

Cradled in turquoise fire

Moments hold still

Earth Mother is in quiet breath

Daughters of Tonantzin

Unfold into painted song

Remembered ancestors

Words carved into hearts rendered

Artists born into healing hands

Poets emerge from angel plumes

My face shaped by bleeding waters

Soul fed in sunlight colors

I have closed my eyes many times

Knowing that I am to be sacrificed

By the waking hour

Skirt of Jade

From the heights of cosmic stone

Descends a momentum gathered by the corners

From the stillness of obsidian skies

The north breaks into shards of smoke

From the spinning of voiceless breath

The west pushes the plumes into a center

From the rumblings that echo into light

The south pours out into drops of jade

From the puddles made from cosmic pools

The east floods into the womb of the sun

Unknown are the depths of conscious souls

Flowers taking root within her skirt of jade

Serpent shimmering from the commotion

Singing labyrinth shedding her skin

Cihuatlampa

Into the surface of Cihuatlampa

Where wisdom goes to be undone

I submerge inside the arms of earthmother

Inside the labyrinth of transformation

I journey in search of new eyes

A necessary evolution

So that to find my way through elevated thoughts

Words meant for those that no longer crawl on their bellies

But sprout into the plumage of resurrected songs

Here I push out from the old skin

Until the decay of fear flakes off

I express life into the currents of water

Nothing must be held

Nothing must be taken

Everything flows through the knowledge of light

Chantico

Dripping jewels break into words

Ancient color studded

Along the throat of nocturnal ambience

Grief moans from behind a cage of bones

Arrogance also is held from speaking

The corridor is vacant from their nuisance

They await for Chantico to kindle the hearth

The labyrinth falls further into night

Into the lost whispers of scented spirits

Of ancestor guides singing

Of unseen rivers painted in turquoise scales

Precious stones of gathered teyolia

Of sleeping malachite made ready for awakening

Altars of obsidian aroused by light

Shadows transform the void into dancing sparks

And there in the sacred pyre

Lie the remnants of flesh and thought

Of which are no longer mine

But sacrificed into the heart of creation

The shedding of seconds invites the moment to flower

Beauty keeps herself within these gentle hands

She is touched by the silence

As the decay of yesterday scales the ground

Pain no longer grips the air of her thoughts

For the infinite of now coils around the apex of the hour

Freedom excites those with souls reborn

Spiral of Renewal

The night sky brushes along the scales

Of earth's glistening skin

Under the moonlight

She appears to be exposed

Her skirt of jade opens

To invite the breath of life

To spin into a coiled conception

An idea of continuous motion

A spiral of renewal

A song feathered in ancient voice

A plumed serpent tattooed with quetzal ink

Bundled in sacred thought

Bathed by both earth and wind

Wisdom born of spirit and flesh

A conduit between life and death

The Feathered Serpent

The truth of divine consciousness

The past

The present

The future

They are One

They are aligned upon a vertical axis

The past is in the earth

Where roots of everything stretch into the heart

The present is at the horizontal plain

Where the flower blooms

The future is hovering above

Where the eagle can see the path

The road that has not yet been walked on

The three levels of existence are not separate

They are connected when in sacred rhythm

You and I have an ability

We can experience any of the three at any moment

This is the truth of our divine nature

Time does not limit us in the present

If I choose to speak to my ancestors

In my heart is where I find them

If I choose to speak to my descendants

From my thoughts I will write them

I am the feathered serpent

I open time

It is creativity that empowers me

Shadows of Deliverance

At the surface

Of waters sculpted in jade

A soothing voice searches

Through vibes unknown

Ruins tremble beneath the belly of ancients past

Upon the floors of bleeding words

Within the veins of time submerged

I am embraced by a wisdom lost

I am found in forgotten thought

Gates of rebirth

Wiped of suffering

Spirit of knowledge jeweled

By the shadows of deliverance

Eyes Renewed

The struggle to transform darkness into light is not ours

We are but mere candles found where most needed

The flame is the truth which has chosen its candle to dwell upon

This truth is not ours but belongs to the Creator

It is the energy within and outside of time

To believe that this force of movement belongs to us

Is the darkness that we have created

Here, the hour sheds from the worn face

Of crumbled stone

The dried scales of minutes

They have forgotten their worth

Inside the moment sliders, time crawls out

Until vacant is left the hollow river bed

The haunting sound of empty chalchihuites

From this emptiness

Wind echoes through the nostrils of my ascent

Feathers have replaced the buried flesh of silence

I am without limits

I am flowing upon the heartbeats of seconds born

Broken is the cycle which gnawed on my hesitation

Released are the voices rescued from stillness

Opened are the eyes through which they now can see

From Fire and Water

Serpent of fire

Serpent of water

Both entwined by reflection

Once unrealized by each other

Summoned by sky

Formed by earth

Mist and ash

The senses decipher the carvings

left upon a sacred heart

An ancient language is learned

As a gentle hand writes

Upon the surface of liquid light

It is here, where my face appears

In the birth stirred by the dream of death

I found awareness

In the wake of shedding skin

Serpent Mother

Coatepec trembles

As a mist of ghosts permeates

From the husks de maíz

From the wounds of a carved serpent

Archaic are the pale scales of gated coils

Yet rebirth awaits within the goddess

I am waking into the slithering crawl

Of voices, of names being spoken by Coatlicue

How many times have I returned

How many faces reflect upon the winding rivers?

How many sunsets have held me

Against the warmth of her bosom?

The Intangible Moment

Ever watch children run

Jump, skip

Wiggle for hours in their freshly made skin

The energy that moves them is authentic

They are told by the spirit that they are unstoppable

This is an intangible moment

But then watch your hands scale

Like leaves corrupted in autumn's song

It is a moment sacrificed

For the sake of laughters recurrence

For the singing of a constant rebirth

Silence whispers from time to time

But it is the dancing

It is the playing

It is what I give which fills in the emptiness

It is my echo within the hollow of the ancient drum

An expression of time in contemplation

Coiled in the shadow of space

An expression of time in the wind of falling leaves

An expression of time in the rising fire of morning light

An expression of time in the rivers of flowing moments

These expressions are simultaneously left behind

And reborn through you and me

As the old skin of the sacred serpent

Makes fertile the primordial womb

Where suns have not yet spoken

Where flowers have not yet bloomed

About the Author

Jorge Montaño is of Mexican and Chilean descent and identifies himself as a Chicano. He was born in the Valle de San Fernando, Califas. Jorge grew up on the Fernandeño-Tataviam land of Pacoima where he studied martial arts until the gang lifestyle shortened any dreams he had of becoming a professional kickboxer. Jorge's views on life then changed from fighting on the streets to a more spiritual perspective. He then found poetry as a form of connecting to the natural order of existing and furthered his calling in the study of metaphors taught by the Tonalpohualli. Jorge learned from all walks of life but the spirit of his poetry mostly draws strength from his indigenous roots. His thirst for knowledge took him upon the path of higher learning, where at the age of 52 he earned an Associate Degree in Chicano Studies. In 2022, Jorge was chosen as the La Raiz Poetry Prize recipient for his poem,

"Sangre Indigena" which was published by La Raiz Magazine and in the 2023 Gente Chicana Edition his poem, "Aqui Estoy", was also chosen for publication by La Raiz Magazine. Jorge credits his poetry to his collaboration with the Spirit of 'In Xochitl, In Cuicatl', which was believed by the Nahuatl people of the pre-Cortez era to be the metaphor for 'the only truth on earth'. He now resides in Santa Barbara where he continues to express his poetry through Flor y Canto.

Instagram Account: @in.tonalli_in.cuicatl

About the Artist

Rick Ortega was born in 1967 in the city of San Fernando, a suburb of Los Angeles, California. He is first generation Mexican American with parents who migrated to the U.S. in the mid 1960's. Rick started creating art at a very young age and would fill up sketch books with pencil drawings of images he was drawn to. In a class field trip to the Getty Museum in Middle school was his first encounter with the old masters that ignited his passion for figurative painting and he has been pursuing that highest level of creativity to this day.

In High School and into college he took classes in art, but it was a Chicano studies coarse that opened a new narrative in his compositions. Learning about the history, myths and legends of Mexico led him to create paintings that were reflective of his history and heritage. In 1997, Mr. Ortega submitted a portfolio of his artwork to The Art Center College of Design in Pasadena CA, where he was awarded a scholarship to attend the prestigious Art school.

Rick Ortega has exhibited his work at Galería de La Raza in San Francisco, National Museum of Mexican Art in Chicago, Art in Embassies in Mexico City, Plaza De La Raza in LA, Museum of Latin American Art in Long Beach, D.A. Center for the Arts in Pomona, Arte Americas in Fresno, Galería Las Americas in Santa Monica, Casa de La Cultura in Las Cruces, Salon 1600 in Topanga, Self Help Graphics in LA, ChimMaya Gallery in Montebello and many other venues and exhibitions throughout Southern California.Rick Ortega was born in 1967 in the city of San Fernando, a suburb of Los Angeles, California. He is first generation Mexican American with parents who migrated to the U.S. in the mid 1960's. Rick started creating art at a very young age and would fill up sketch books with pencil drawings of images he was drawn to. In a class field trip to the Getty Museum in Middle school was his first encounter with the old masters that ignited his passion for figurative painting and he has been pursuing that highest level of creativity to this day.

In High School and into college he took classes in art, but it was a Chicano studies coarse that opened a new narrative in his compositions. Learning about the history, myths and legends of Mexico led him to create paintings that were reflective of his history and heritage. In 1997, Mr. Ortega submitted a portfolio of his artwork to The Art Center College of Design in Pasadena CA, where he was awarded a scholarship to attend the prestigious Art school.

Rick Ortega has exhibited his work at Galería de La Raza in San Francisco, National Museum of Mexican Art in Chicago, Art in Embassies in Mexico City, Plaza De La Raza in LA, Museum of Latin American Art in Long Beach, D.A. Center for the Arts in Pomona, Arte Americas in Fresno, Galería Las Americas in Santa Monica, Casa de La Cultura in Las Cruces, Salon 1600 in Topanga, Self Help Graphics in LA, ChimMaya Gallery in Montebello and many other venues and exhibitions throughout Southern California.

About the Publisher

Riot of Roses Publishing House was founded in 2021 specifically to amplify the stories of historically silenced voices and narratives. Xicana owned. Mujerista focused. For the people.

We publish books that heal and liberate.

Read our rebellion.

RIOT OF ROSES
PUBLISHING HOUSE
SEJATNGA
UNCEDED TONGVA TERRITORY
SOUTH WHITTIER, CALIFORNIA

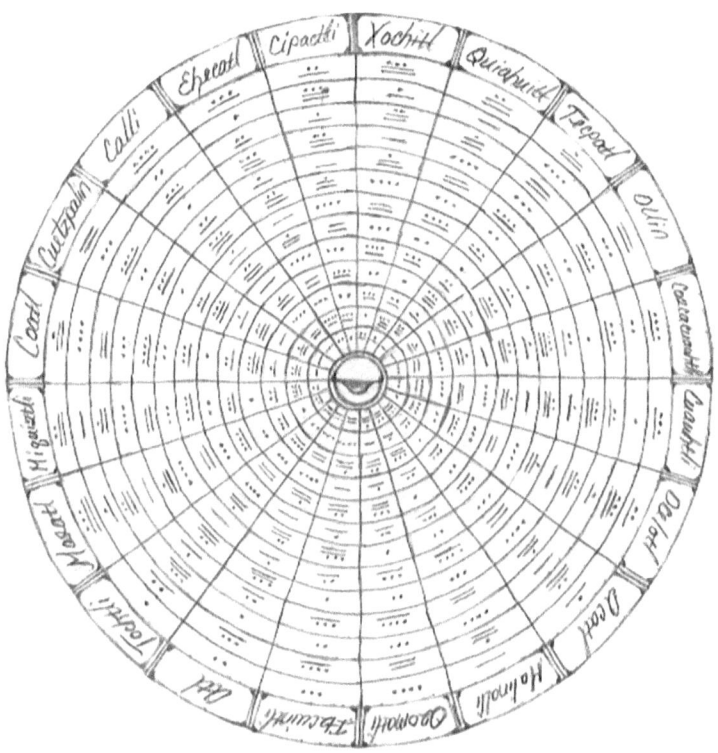

www.ingramcontent.com/pod-product-compliance
Lightning Source LLC
Chambersburg PA
CBHW030914140626
46545CB00017B/2351